DISCOVERING CAREERS FOR YOUR FUTURE

teaching

Ferguson Publishing Company
Chicago, Illinois

Carol Yehling
Editor

Beth Adler, Herman Adler Design Group
Cover design

Carol Yehling
Interior design

Bonnie Needham
Proofreader

Library of Congress Cataloging-in-Publication Data

Discovering careers for your future. Teaching.
        p. cm.
   Includes index.
   ISBN 0-89434-398-X
1. Teaching—Vocational guidance—United States—Juvenile literature. 2. Teachers—Training of—United States—Juvenile literature. [1. Teaching—Vocational guidance. 2. Vocational guidance.] I. Title: Teaching. II. Ferguson Publishing Company.

LB1775.2 .D58 2001
371.1'0023'73—dc21

                         2001033079

Published and distributed by
Ferguson Publishing Company
200 West Jackson Boulevard, 7th Floor
Chicago, Illinois 60606
800-306-9941
www.fergpubco.com

Printed in the United States of America
Y-9

Table of Contents

Introduction

You may not have decided yet what you want to be in the future. And you don't have to decide right away. You do know that right now you are interested in teaching. Do any of the statements below describe you? If so, you may want to begin thinking about what a career in education might mean for you.

___I enjoy going to school every day.
___I have leadership qualities.
___I am good at explaining things to other people.
___I enjoy baby-sitting and being with young children.
___I am good at public speaking.
___I like to lead discussions.
___I am interested in learning new things every day.
___I like to get other people interested in my hobbies (music, sports, computers, or photography, for example).
___I enjoy homework assignments that involve preparing oral presentations.
___If I learn something quickly in class, I am eager to help my classmates understand.

Discovering Careers for Your Future: Teaching is a book about careers in education, from adult and vocational education teachers to teacher aides. Teachers of younger students usually teach a wide variety of subjects and skills, including reading, writing, math, and getting along with others. Teachers of older students tend to specialize in one subject, such as math or history. College-level teachers may specialize even more and teach only American history or African-American history. Some teachers focus on educating a special group of people, such as people with disabilities, or those who don't speak English. Teachers do not work just in schools, but in businesses, industries, museums, and parks. Some teachers become interested in the education process and work in administration and planning.

This book describes many possibilities for future careers in teaching. Read through it and see how the different careers are connected. For example, if you are interested in young children, you will want to read the chapters on Child Care Workers, Elementary School Teachers, ESL Teachers, Preschool Teachers, Special Education Teachers, and Teacher Aides. If you are interested in teaching adults, you will want to read the chapters on Adult and Vocational Education Teachers, Athletic Trainers, Career Counselors, and College Professors. Go ahead and explore!

What do teachers do?

The first section of each chapter begins with a heading such as "What School Administrators Do" or "What Education Directors Do." It tells what it's like to work at this job. It describes typical responsibilities and assignments. You will find out about working conditions. Which teachers work in traditional classrooms? Which ones work in nontraditional settings? This section answers all these questions.

How do I become a teacher?

The section called "Education and Training" tells you what schooling you need for employment in each job—a high school diploma, training at a junior college, a college degree, or more. It also talks about on-the-job training that you could expect to receive after you're hired, and whether or not you must complete an apprenticeship program.

How much do teachers earn?

The "Earnings" section gives the average salary figures for the job described in the chapter. These figures give you a general idea of how much money people with this job can make. Keep in mind that many people really earn more or less than the amounts given here because actual salaries depend on many different things, such as the size of the company, the location of the company, and the amount of education, training, and experience you have. Generally, but not always, bigger companies located in major cities pay more than smaller ones in smaller cities and towns, and people with more education, training, and experience earn more. Also remember that these figures are current averages. They will probably be different by the time you are ready to enter the workforce.

What will the future be like for teachers?

The "Outlook" section discusses the employment outlook for the career: whether the total number of people employed in this career will increase or decrease in the coming years and whether jobs in this field will be easy or hard to find. These predictions are based on economic conditions, the size and makeup of the population, foreign competition, and new technology. Terms such as "faster than the average," "about as fast as the average," and "slower than the average," are terms used by the U.S. Department of Labor to describe job growth predicted by government data.

Keep in mind that these predictions are general statements. No one knows for sure what the future will be like. Also remember that the employment outlook is a general statement about an industry and does not necessarily apply to everyone. A determined and talented person may be able to find a job in an industry or career with the worst kind of outlook. And a person without ambition and the proper training will find it difficult to find a job in even a booming industry or career field.

Where can I find more information?

Each chapter includes a sidebar called "For More Info." It lists organizations that you can contact to find out more about the field and careers in the field. You will find names, addresses, phone numbers, and Web sites.

Extras

Every chapter has a few extras. There are photos that show teachers in action. There are sidebars and notes on ways to explore the field, related jobs, fun facts, profiles of people in the field, or lists of Web sites and books that might be helpful. At the end of the book you will find a glossary and an index. The glossary gives brief definitions of words that relate to education, career training, or employment that you may be unfamiliar with. The index includes all the job titles mentioned in the book. It is followed by a list of general teaching Web sites.

It's not too soon to think about your future. We hope you discover several possible career choices. Happy hunting!

Adult and Vocational Education Teachers

What Adult and Vocational Education Teachers Do

Adult and vocational education teachers teach classes for adults and high school students. Older students take classes to prepare for better jobs or for advanced education. They might take courses to improve skills they already have or to learn new technologies. Adult education teachers lead classes, assign reading, and help students develop technical and academic skills.

Adult education teachers in basic education programs teach students school subjects like English, math, and composition. In vocational training programs, they teach trades such as automobile repair or carpentry. They also work within companies, training employees for specific job positions. In community colleges, they teach subjects as varied as airplane flying, computer programming, foreign language, and oil painting.

Adult education teachers must enjoy the subject they teach and communicate their enthusiasm to their students.

Adult education teachers may teach one person at a time or a large classroom of students. Classes may take place in a laboratory, a shop, or at actual work sites. Adult and vocational education teachers prepare for classes the same as any other kind of teacher. They decide what books and other learning materials to use. They prepare a daily schedule, give lectures, and lead class discussions. They prepare and give exams, and grade essays and presentations. Some industries require teachers to cover specific subjects and students must pass strict industry tests before they are qualified for certain positions.

EXPLORING

• Volunteer to tutor peers or younger students. Your school or community center may have volunteer tutoring opportunities.

• Volunteer to assist in special educational activities at nursing homes, churches, or community centers. For example, you might be able to teach senior citizens how to use the Internet or teach a foreign student to speak English.

Education and Training

Adult education teachers usually focus on a specific subject. They become teachers because of their expertise gained through education, on-the-job training, work experience, and personal interest.

In most states, teachers of adult basic education must have a bachelor's degree in education. Some states also require a teaching certificate. Vocational instructors need to have practical experience in the skills they are teaching. Some professions require vocational teachers in their field to have a teaching license or certificate. For some subjects teachers need no special certification or training in education, but they need to be extremely knowledgeable in their field.

THE TOP 10

These are the top 10 certificates and associate's degrees awarded by community colleges in the 1996-97 academic year, according to the National Center for Education Statistics.

Certificate	Number Awarded
Health professions and related sciences	56,659
Business management and administrative services	24,176
Mechanics and repairs	14,888
Protective services	13,507
Precision production trades	9,486
Vocational home economics	7,595
Personal and miscellaneous services	6,744
Engineering-related technologies	6,203
Construction trades	5,544
Transportation and material moving workers	4,935

Associate Degree	Number Awarded
Liberal/general studies and humanities	167,448
Health professions and related sciences	76,848
Business management and administrative services	71,766
Engineering-related technologies	20,208
Protective services	17,445
Mechanics and repairs	9,747
Education	9,687
Visual and performing arts	8,757
Multi/interdisciplinary studies	8,246
Computer and information sciences	7,701

Earnings

Full-time adult and vocational education teachers earn an average of $34,430 a year. In general, full-time instructors earn between $24,890 and $45,230 a year, with some highly skilled and experienced teachers earning more. Earnings vary widely according to the subject, the number of courses taught, the teacher's experience, and the location.

About half of all adult and vocational education teachers teach part-time. They are often paid by the hour. Hourly rates range from $6 to $50.

FOR MORE INFO

American Association for Adult and Continuing Education
1200 19th Street, NW, Suite 300
Washington, DC 20036
202-429-5131
http://www.aaace.org

American Vocational Association
1410 King Street
Alexandria, VA 22314
800-826-9972
http://avaonline.org

For information about government programs, contact:
U.S. Department of Education
Office of Vocational and Adult Education
400 Maryland Avenue, SW
Washington, DC 20202
202-205-5451
http://www.ed.gov/offices/ovae

Outlook

Employment opportunities in adult education are expected to grow as fast as the average through 2008. Adults know they need to keep learning to succeed and advance in today's workplace. In fact, many courses are paid for by companies that want their employees trained in the latest skills and technology of their field. The biggest growth areas will be in computer technology, automotive mechanics, and medical technology. Major employers of adult and vocational education teachers will be vocational high schools, private trade schools, community colleges, and private adult education enterprises.

Athletic Trainers

What Athletic Trainers Do

Athletic trainers help athletes stay healthy and avoid injuries. They work with injured athletes to get them back into competitive shape. The professional athletic trainer may work with a team of physicians, physical therapists, and dietitians to plan a program of health maintenance for team athletes. Their main purpose is to keep the athletes competitive and fit. The trainer's program includes exercise, weight lifting, relaxation and meditation, and controlled diet.

If an athlete is injured, the trainer is in charge of treating the injury and helping the athlete recover completely. Athletic trainers work with physicians and coaches to decide if the athlete should continue to compete or not. Where the athlete is to compete, how important the event, and how extensive the injury are all factors in the decision. A trainer may decide to let a runner continue training with a sprained ankle if the Olympics trials are days away. If there is only a small competition coming up, the trainer may recommend that the athlete take a few weeks off to recover. The trainer designs a series of exercises that rebuild strength without damaging or straining the injured area.

Athletic trainers work hard to prevent injuries. They recommend running, stretching, weight lifting, and other exercise programs to help athletes stay in good physical condition and make their bodies stronger. Athletic trainers may also design workout programs to strengthen weaker body parts, such as ankles and elbows, to reduce the likelihood of injury.

During competition, trainers treat minor injuries, such as cuts and bruises. They use ice, bandages, and other first aid to reduce swelling and help athletes cope with pain. For more serious injuries, such as a bad sprain or broken bone, trainers make sure that the athletes receive proper medical attention.

Trainers use hot baths, massage, whirlpool treatment, wrapping injured areas, and other techniques to speed the athlete's recovery.

EXPLORING

• Participate in school and community sports programs.

• Take classes in first aid and CPR. Check with your local American Heart Association or Red Cross chapter for course schedules.

• Participate in physical fitness programs offered at your YMCA/ YWCA, park district, or local gym. Try different types of training, including aerobics, weight training, and stretching.

• Learn about nutrition and how diet affects both physical performance and mental stamina.

FACTS ABOUT INJURIES TO HIGH SCHOOL ATHLETES

More than half of injuries to high school athletes in nine sports were found to occur during practice sessions, according to a study released by the National Athletic Trainers' Association (NATA). The sports studied were baseball (boys), softball (girls), football (boys), field hockey (girls), soccer (both), basketball (both), volleyball (girls), and wrestling (boys). The data came from 246 certified athletic trainers representing different-sized schools across the country. The results of this study showed these discoveries:

• Football had the highest rate of injuries, while volleyball showed the lowest rate.

• The largest number of fractures came from boys' baseball, basketball, soccer, and softball, in that order.

• More than 73 percent of injuries required players to stop competing fewer than eight days.

• The highest frequency of knee injuries occurred in girls' soccer.

• The largest proportion of surgeries reported among the 10 sports was for girls' basketball and the lowest was field hockey. Most of the injuries requiring surgery were knee injuries.

Education and Training

To become an athletic trainer you need a bachelor's degree in physical education, physical therapy, or another area related to health care. Trainers should take courses in first aid, anatomy, nutrition, and physical therapy in addition to general courses in health and the sciences, especially biology and chemistry.

Trainers can earn a certificate from the National Athletic Trainers' Association (NATA). You must pass an examination and have at least two years of experience working under the supervision of an NATA-certified trainer.

Earnings

Beginning athletic trainers earn about $25,000 a year. Trainers who work with college athletes earn slightly more. Trainers for professional teams earn between $40,000 and $80,000 a year. Some trainers work all year and others work only during the playing season. Trainers who work for schools usually earn a teacher's salary plus an additional amount for their training duties.

Outlook

As sports continue to grow in popularity, there should be a need for more skilled athletic trainers. However, many people want to enter this field, so those with the best education and training will have the most success finding a job. Trainers who want to work for professional sports teams will face the most job competition but will also earn the highest salaries. A master's degree is usually required to gain these top positions.

FOR MORE INFO

**American Sports
Medicine Association**
2141 K Street, NW
Washington, DC 20037
202-223-2468
http://www.americansma.com

**American Athletic Trainers'
Association Board of Certification**
1512 South 143rd Circle
Omaha, NE 68137
402-559-0091
http://www.nataboc.org

**National Athletic
Trainers' Association**
2952 Stemmons Freeway, Suite 200
Dallas, TX 75247-6196
214-637-6282
http://www.nata.org

RELATED JOBS

Aerobics Instructors and Fitness Trainers
Physical Therapists
Physical Therapy Assistants
Sports Physicians

Career Counselors

Why Someone Might Need a Career Counselor

Layoffs

Relocation

Technological advances that change work tasks

No advancement opportunities

Divorce

Retirement

Insufficient salary

Change in interests

Job dissatisfaction

Prison release

What Career Counselors Do

Career counselors help people discover their occupational interests and skills and guide them in career decisions. First, counselors get to know their clients and what their goals, abilities, and interests are. Counselors sometimes give tests, including achievement and aptitude tests. The results of the tests and personal interviews with the clients help career counselors identify possible career choices for them.

Counselors suggest education and training programs if the client needs them. They teach job-hunting strategies, such as responding to newspaper ads, doing Internet searches, and sending out resumes and cover letters. Counselors might teach interview tactics, and how to discuss salary and benefits with potential employers.

Employment counselors might also work with employers to help them hire people for specific job openings. They gather descriptions of the particular positions that employers need to fill and find qualified candidates for employers to interview.

Career counselors have enormous responsibilities as they assist people in making major life decisions. They need thorough knowledge of education, training, employment trends, the job market, and career resources.

Education and Training

To be a career counselor you must usually have a master's degree and complete a period of supervised counseling before you can practice on your own. A doctorate is generally recommended for the best jobs. New career counselors are often considered trainees for the first six months to a year of their employment. They may work for schools, colleges, or public health agencies, in business and industry, or have their own private practices.

To become certified by the National Board of Certified Counselors, career counselors must have at least a master's degree in counseling (or a related field, such as psy-

EXPLORING

• Learn library skills, such as researching, cataloging, and filing.

• Look at the Help Wanted section of your newspaper. Most newspapers run these ads every day and have an expanded job section on Sundays. If you live in a small city or town, you might want to take a look at a newspaper from a large city, such as New York, Chicago, or Los Angeles. Choose some job categories that interest you and find out what the typical education, experience, and personal requirements are for jobs in that category.

• Explore Internet job-search sites like Monster (http://www.monster.com) and HotJobs (http://www.hotjobs.com).

CAREER COUNSELING TIMELINE

- The first funded employment office in the United States was established in San Francisco in 1886.

- In 1908, the Civic Service House in Boston began the first program of vocational guidance, and the Vocational Bureau was established to help young people choose, train, and enter appropriate careers.

- In 1910, a national conference on vocational guidance was held in Boston. The federal government gave support to vocational counseling by initiating a program to assist veterans of World War I in readjusting to civilian life.

- During the Great Depression, agencies such as the Civilian Conservation Corps and the National Youth Administration offered vocational counseling.

- On June 6, 1933, the Wagner-Pyser Act established the United States Employment Service. States came into the service one by one, with each state developing its own plan under the prescribed limits of the act.

- By the end of World War II, the Veterans Administration was counseling more than 50,000 veterans each month.

- State and federal government agencies now involved with vocational guidance services include the Bureau of Indian Affairs, the Bureau of Apprenticeship and Training, the Office of Manpower Development, and the Department of Education.

chology), experience as a supervised counselor, and a minimum of three years of full-time independent career counseling.

Earnings

Salaries vary greatly within the career and vocational counseling field. Median salaries for full-time educational and vocational counselors were $36,650 in 1998, according to the U.S. Department of Labor. Salaries ranged from less than $21,200 to more than $73,900. Those in business or industry can earn higher salaries.

Outlook

There should be good growth in the field of employment counseling through 2008, according to the U.S. Department of Labor. Opportunities for employment and rehabilitation counselors in state and local governments will not grow as rapidly as jobs in human resource and employment assistance programs in private business and industry.

FOR MORE INFO

Career Planning and Adult Development Network
PO Box 1484
Pacifica, CA 94044
650-359-6911
http://www.careernetwork.org/

National Board for Certified Counselors
3 Terrace Way, Suite D
Greensboro, NC 27403-3660
336-547-0607
http://www.nbcc.org

National Career Development Association
10820 East 45th Street, Suite 210
Tulsa, OK 74146
918-663-7060
http://ncda.org

RELATED JOBS

Employment Firm Workers
Guidance Counselors
Personnel and Labor
Relations Specialists
Rehabilitation Counselors
Social Workers

Child Care Workers

What Child Care Workers Do

Child care workers work with infants, toddlers, and preschool-aged children at day care centers, preschools, or other child care facilities. While parents and guardians are at work, they watch young children and help them develop skills through games and activities. They make sure babies are fed, diapered, and held when awake. They teach toddlers how to tie their shoes and button their coats and how to get along with other children.

Child care workers at larger centers may have more structured activities. They read to the children, guide arts and crafts projects, and teach them songs. They help preschoolers develop basic skills, such as recognizing letters, numbers, and colors. Child care workers lead children in simple tasks, such as cleaning up after themselves, picking up toys, and washing their hands.

A child care worker's job is mainly supervising children at indoor and outdoor play, making sure they are safe, happy, and well taken care of. They should know basic first aid and be able to react quickly in emergency situations. Child care workers provide a nutritious midday meal and occasional snacks. They also make sure children take naps or have quiet times during the day.

Child care workers must follow the wishes of parents. They provide parents with reports on their children's progress and behavior and notify them immediately if there are any problems. It is just as important to have a good relationship with the parents as it is to get along with the children.

Education and Training

In high school, you should take child development, home economics, and other classes that involve you with child care. You should also take courses in English, art, music, and theater to develop creative skills.

To be a child care worker, you need a high school diploma and some child care experience. Requirements vary among employers, though. Some employers pre-

EXPLORING

• There are many volunteer opportunities that will give you experience in working with children. Check with your library or local literacy program about tutoring children and reading to preschoolers. Summer day camps, church schools, children's theaters, museums, and other organizations with children's programs may also need volunteer assistants.

• Talk to neighbors, relatives, and others with small children about baby-sitting evenings and weekends.

RELATED JOBS

Elementary School Teachers
Guidance Counselors
Preschool Teachers
Special Education Teachers
Teacher Aides

fer to hire workers who have taken college courses in child development, or hold bachelor's degrees. You may earn better wages if you have some college education. Certification isn't required of child care workers, but you can earn a certificate from some organizations, such as the Council for Early Childhood Professional Recognition or the National Child Care Association.

Earnings

According to the U.S. Department of Labor, child care workers earned about $6.60 an hour in 1998, which amounts to yearly earnings of about $13,750 for full-time work. Salaries range from

SAFETY CONCERNS FOR KIDS

CRIBS: Older cribs and mattresses that are too small can cause strangulation and suffocation. Cribs must meet current national safety standards and be in good condition. Crib slats should be no more than 2 3/8" apart and mattresses should fit snugly.

BEDDING: Sudden Infant Death Syndrome (SIDS) and suffocation is sometimes related to the use of pillows, soft bedding, or comforters. Babies should be put to sleep on their backs in a crib with a firm, flat mattress.

PLAYGROUND SURFACES: Children can suffer injuries from falls, especially head injuries, when playground surfaces are too hard. Outdoor playgrounds should have at least 12 inches of wood chips, mulch, sand, or pea gravel, or mats made of safety-tested rubber or rubber-like materials.

SAFETY GATES: Safety gates, especially on stairs, can protect against many hazards, especially falls.

WINDOW BLIND AND CURTAIN CORDS: Children can be strangled in the loops of window blind and curtain cords. Miniblinds and Venetian blinds should not have looped cords. Vertical blinds, continuous looped blinds, and drapery cords should have tension or tie-down devices to hold the cords tight.

CLOTHING DRAWSTRINGS: Drawstrings can catch on playground and other equipment and strangle young children. Be sure there are no drawstrings around the hood and neck of children's outer-wear clothing. Other types of clothing fasteners, like snaps, zippers, or hook and loop fasteners (such as Velcro), should be used instead.

$11,400 or less to $20,070 a year.

Outlook

Employment of child care workers should increase faster than the average through 2008. Many positions open up because these workers don't stay in their jobs very long. One of the main reasons for this is the low pay.

More child care centers, both nonprofit and for-profit, are expected to open in the next few years as more mothers take jobs outside the home and need child care services. There will be more jobs available with franchises and national chains, as well as centers that cater exclusively to corporate employees. Bilingual child care workers will find more job opportunities and better salaries. The Children's Defense Fund reports that three out of five preschoolers in the United States are in child care.

FOR MORE INFO

National Association for the Education of Young Children
1509 16th Street, NW
Washington, DC 20036
800-424-2460
http://www.naeyc.org

Council for Early Childhood Professional Recognition
2460 16th Street, NW
Washington, DC 20009-3575
800-424-4310
http://www.cdacouncil.org

For information about student memberships and training opportunities, contact:
National Association of Child Care Professionals
PO Box 90723
Austin, TX 78709-0723
512-301-5557
http://www.naccp.org

For information about certification and to learn about the issues affecting child care, contact:
National Child Care Association
1016 Rosser Street
Conyers, GA 30012
800-543-7161
http://www.nccanet.org

College Administrators

Who's in Charge?

College administrators include:

Vice presidents of business, student services, or academic affairs

Controllers

Directors of housing

Physical plant directors

Directors of human resources

Student activities directors

Admissions directors

Financial aid directors

Directors of security and safety

Directors of purchasing

College union directors

Directors of food services

What College Administrators Do

College administrators develop and manage services for students in colleges and universities. Administrators arrange housing; special services for veterans, minorities, and students with disabilities; and social, cultural, and recreational activities. The most common administrators are presidents, deans, registrars, and directors of student activities.

College *presidents* are the top administrators. Their duties include overseeing academic programs, planning budgets, hiring and firing faculty and other staff, and fund-raising.

The *dean of students* heads the entire student-affairs program. Associate or assistant deans may be in charge of specific aspects of student life such as housing. Academic deans handle such issues as course offerings or faculty.

Registrars prepare class schedules, make room assignments, keep records of students and their grades, and gather data for government and educational agencies.

The *director of student activities* helps student groups plan and arrange social, cultural, and recreational events. Other student-affairs administrators include the *director of housing,* who manages room assignments and the upkeep of dormitory buildings. *Directors of religious activities* coordinate the activities of various religious groups.

Foreign-student advisors work with foreign students and give special help with admissions, housing, financial aid, and English instruction. The *director of the student health program* hires staff and manages the health care center and its equipment. *Athletic directors* are in charge of all intercollegiate athletic activities. They hire coaches, schedule sports events, and direct publicity efforts.

Education and Training

To be a college administrator, you need a well-rounded education that prepares you for college. For most college administration jobs, you need at least a bachelor's degree. For the top positions you need a

EXPLORING

• Work in student government positions or serve as chair for clubs you belong to. You will get both management and administrative experience.

• Familiarize yourself with all the various aspects of college life by looking at college student handbooks and course catalogs (available at your library). Most handbooks list all the offices and administrators and how they assist students and faculty.

The median salary of college administrators continues to increase at a faster rate than inflation. The Consumer Price Index showed that inflation increased 3.4 percent in 2000. College administrator salaries increased 4.8 percent in the 2000-01 academic year, according to an annual survey by the College and University Professional Association for Human Resources.

The survey also showed these salary increases:

- A 5.9 percent increase at specialized institutions (like fine-arts schools)

- A 5.2 percent increase at doctoral institutions

- A 5.0 percent increase at comprehensive institutions

- A 4.2 percent increase at two-year institutions

- A 4.1 percent increase at baccalaureate institutions

master's or doctoral degree in administration, business, or education. In addition to a degree, you must have many years of experience at a college or university as a lower-level administrator, professor, or department chair, for example.

Earnings

Salaries vary greatly for college deans and related workers and depend on the college's location, whether it is a two-year or four-year institution, and whether it is public or private. Most of the jobs described above pay salaries that average from $32,000 to $45,000 a year. University presidents make the highest salaries, followed by deans of students and athletic directors. Deans earn from $70,000 a year to well over $200,000 a year, depending on the school and the department.

According to the 1997-98 Administrative Compensation Survey conducted by tne

College and University Professional Association for Human Resources, the median salary for deans of medicine is $235,000 a year, while the median annual salary for deans of nursing is $76,380.

Outlook

The number of college-age students is expected to increase, so more jobs may open in the field. However, leaner budgets are currently making the job market in college administration competitive. Most job openings will be to replace workers who are retiring or leaving their jobs.

The U.S. Department of Labor predicts there will be strong competition for college administrator positions. Most administrative jobs are filled by faculty who have gained the educational and experience requirements needed. Budget problems have forced some colleges and universities to reduce administrative jobs.

FOR MORE INFO

American Association of University Administrators
2602 Rutford Avenue
Richardson, TX 75080-1470
972-248-3957
http://www.aaua.org

Association of College Administration Professionals
PO Box 1389
Staunton, VA 24402
540-885-1873
http://www.acap.org

College and University Professional Association for Human Resources
1233 20th Street, NW, Suite 301
Washington, DC 20036-1250
202-429-0311
http://www.cupahr.org

RELATED JOBS

Adult and Vocational Education Teachers
College Professors
Guidance Counselors
School Administrators

College Professors

What College Professors Do

College and university faculty instruct students at two-year and four-year colleges and universities. *College professors* have three main responsibilities: teaching, advising, and conducting research. Teaching is the most important. Professors give lectures, lead discussions, give exams, and assign textbook reading and term papers. They may spend fewer than 10 hours a week in the classroom, but they spend many hours preparing lectures and lesson plans, grading papers and exams, and preparing grade reports. They also meet with students individually outside of the classroom to guide them in the course, and keep them updated about their progress.

Some faculty members also work as student advisers, helping students decide which courses to take, informing them of requirements for their majors, and directing them toward scholarships and other

Professors may lecture in small classrooms or large auditoria, depending on the size of the university and the popularity of their courses.

financial aid. They may also help students adjust to college life, and guide them through difficult problems.

Many college professors conduct research in their field of study and publish the results in textbooks and journals. They attend conferences and present research findings to professors from other universities. They employ graduate students as assistants both in research projects and in teaching.

Education and Training

During your middle- and high-school years, you should concentrate on a col-

EXPLORING

• Talk to your teachers about their careers and their college experiences.
• Volunteer with a community center, day care center, or summer camp to get teaching experience.
• Look at course catalogs and read about the faculty members and the courses they teach. These are available at your library.

lege preparatory program and focus on your particular interest. When you finish your undergraduate degree and enter a master's program, you will probably be required to take on some assistant-teaching responsibilities.

To teach in a college or university, you must have at least a master's degree. With a master's degree you can become an instructor. You will need a doctorate for a job as an assistant professor, which is the entry-level job title for college faculty. Faculty members usually spend

no more than six years as assistant professors. During this time, the college will decide whether to grant you tenure, which is a type of job security, and promote you to associate professor. An associate professor may eventually be promoted to full professor.

Earnings

Full professors at public universities earn an average of about $70,000 a year, while professors at private universities receive about $85,000 a year. Associate professors earn an average of $50,000 annually at public universities, and $56,000 at private.

The *Chronicle of Higher Education* conducts an annual survey of the salaries of college professors. The 1998 survey found that full professors at public universities earned average salaries of about $70,000 a year and professors at private universities earned $85,000 a year. Associate professors received an average of $50,000 annually at public universities, and $57,000 at private ones. For assistant professors, the average salaries were $42,000 at public universities and $47,000 at private ones.

Professors working in the western Pacific states, such as California and Oregon, earned the most, followed by those working in New England. The survey found the average pay to be the lowest in such southern states as Alabama, Kentucky, and Mississippi.

FOR MORE INFO

American Federation of Teachers
555 New Jersey Avenue, NW
Washington, DC 20001
202-879-4400
http://www.aft.org

**American Association
of University Professors**
1012 14th Street, NW Suite 500
Washington, DC 20005
202-737-5900
http://www.aaup.org

Outlook

The U.S. Department of Labor says there should be faster than average growth for college and university professors through 2008. College enrollment is expected to rise from 14.6 million in 1998 to 16.1 million in 2008. Competition will be especially strong for full-time, tenure-track positions at four-year universities. Opportunities for college teachers will be good in engineering, business, computer science, and health science.

Computer Trainers

What Computer Trainers Do

Today's employees and students need to know how to send email, how to use the Internet, and how to use word processing programs. However, many people become frustrated when faced with a blank computer screen and a thick instruction manual. Sometimes, too, the computers and programs are too complex to be explained fully and clearly by a manual. *Computer trainers* teach people how to use computers, software, and other new technology. When a business installs new hardware and software, computer trainers work one-on-one with the employees, or they lead group training sessions. They may also offer instruction over the Internet. With technology changing every day, computer trainers are called upon often for support and instruction.

Computer trainers teach people how to use computer programs. For example a company's accounting department may

Carnegie-Mellon University

Computer trainers must know their subject backwards and forwards in order to answer questions from both beginning and advanced students.

need a computer trainer to teach its accounting clerks how to use a spreadsheet program, which is used to make graphs and charts, and to calculate sums. Other common business programs include database programs, which keep track of such things as customer names, addresses, and phone numbers, and word processing programs, which are used to create documents, letters, and reports. Some computer trainers may also teach computer programming languages such as C or Visual Basic.

Many corporations, advertisers, and individuals have set up home pages on the Internet. A computer trainer can help them use the language needed to design a page, and teach them how to update the page. Trainers teach people how to operate desktop publishing programs and laser printers that allow individuals and

EXPLORING

• Use your library, bookstores, and the Internet to keep up with the latest software and technology. The Internet has thousands of sites on computers and computer training.

• Teach yourself as many software packages as you can.

• Teach new programs to your parents, grandparents, or younger sisters and brothers.

businesses to create interesting graphics and full-color pages for brochures and newsletters. Some computer trainers may also help offices set up their own office network. With a network, all the computers in an office can be linked. Employees then share programs and files, conference with other employees, and send electronic mail.

Computer trainers may be self-employed and work on a freelance basis, or they may work for a computer training school or computer service company.

Education and Training

Most community colleges, universities, and vocational schools offer computer courses. Computer service companies and training schools also offer courses in specific software programs. Though college courses and training are important, it helps to have experience, too. You can get experience by working with computers on a regular basis, either at home or in the work place. Computer experience can also come from working in the sales

THE HISTORY OF COMPUTING ON THE WEB

IEEE Computer Society History of Computing
http://www.computer.org/history

The Virtual Museum of Computing
http://xlmp.museophile.com/computing.html

Past Notable Women of Computing
http://www.cs.yale.edu/homes/tap/past-women-cs.html

department of a computer store or software company.

Education requirements vary at computer training schools and computer service companies. To work as a teacher in a high school or community college, a bachelor's degree is the minimum requirement.

Earnings

The average training specialist earns about $40,300. Senior training specialists average $47,400 a year, and training managers earn about $57,000. In general, salaries for computer trainers increase with the level of education.

Computer trainers often earn yearly bonuses. In 1996, bonuses for training specialists averaged $1,600, senior training specialists received $2,500, and training managers were awarded $5,200 on average.

Outlook

The outlook for computer trainers is excellent through 2008

FOR MORE INFO

The American Society for Training and Development
1640 King Street, Box 1443
Alexandria, VA 22313-2043
http://www.astd.org

International Association of Information Technology Trainers
PMB 4516030-M Marshalee Drive
Elkridge, MD 21075-5935
410-290-7000
http://www.itrain.org

because more people are using computers than ever before.

Information from the EQW National Employer Survey says that more employers are using a variety of outside training providers. According to the American Society of Training and Development, the short life cycles of technology products, combined with the greater complexity of many job roles, will increase the demand for computer trainers.

Education Directors

Read All About It

From Knowledge to Narrative: Educators and the Changing Museum by Lisa C. Roberts (Smithsonian Institution, 1997).

Learning from Museums: Visitor Experiences and the Making of Meaning by John H. Falk and Lynn D. Dierking (Altamira Press, 2000).

Learning in the Museum by George E. Hein (Routledge, 1998).

What Education Directors Do

Education directors help museums and zoo visitors learn more about the exhibits they have come to see. Education directors plan and develop educational programs. These programs include tours, lectures, and classes that focus on the history or environment of a particular artifact or animal.

For example, a museum or zoo might focus on helping children understand more about the exhibits. In museums, children often are allowed to handle artifacts or play with objects. In zoos, children may be able to pet animals. Education directors develop special projects to help visitors learn more from this type of hands-on experience.

Education directors give teachers advice in how to lead workshops and classes. They help resource directors find materials, such as egg shells or skeletons, and instruments, such as microscopes, to use in their resource centers. They work with exhibit designers to create displays, perhaps showing the development of a moth into a butterfly, or display tools and artifacts used by ancient Egyptians. They also work with graphic designers to produce signs and illustrations that reveal more about an exhibit. Signs in a gorilla exhibit, for instance, may include a map of Africa to show where gorillas live.

Most education directors at museums work in art, history, or science, but other museums have a special interest, such as woodcarvings or circuses. These directors must have some training or experience in special fields, just as those at zoos must know about animals. Wherever they work, education directors must have a good knowledge of all the specimens in their collection.

Education and Training

Education directors usually begin in another position at a zoo or museum, perhaps as a teacher or resource coordinator. They are usually promoted into the position, or transfer between organizations to reach the director level. Education directors must have at least a bachelor's degree. Most positions require a master's

EXPLORING

• Most zoos and museums have student volunteers. Volunteers often help with tours, organize files or audiovisual materials, or assist a lecturer in a class.

• The American Association of Museums publishes an annual museum directory, a monthly newsletter, and a bimonthly magazine. It also published *Museum Careers: A Variety of Vocations, Resource Report 2, Part I*, in 1988. This report is helpful for anyone considering a career in the museum field.

• *Introduction to Museum Work* by George Ellis Burcaw, published in 1983 by the American Association for State and Local History, discusses the educational programs at various museums.

A DAY IN THE LIFE OF AN EDUCATION DIRECTOR

7:30—Arrive at the museum. Check in at the security station and pick up identification badge.

7:45—Settle in office. Return phone calls and email.

9:00—Attend meeting with anthropology and history curators, exhibit designers, and museum taxidermist. Discuss plans for upcoming exhibit. Focus on exhibit design that will best represent objects and include thought-provoking interpretation for museum visitors.

10:30—Give tour of rainforest exhibit to second graders.

12:00—Give lunch lecture on Native American cradleboards to Civic Foundation members.

1:00—Lunch

1:30—Give tour of Egyptian exhibit to high school students.

2:45—Meet with education staff to develop ideas for instructional materials to use with the upcoming exhibit. Focus on materials for self-guided tours, families, and teachers.

4:15—Return phone calls and email messages. Open mail.

5:15—Prepare budget material for tomorrow's meeting with the director of finance and the museum director.

6:00—Stop at the security station and turn in badge.

degree, and many, including those at larger zoos and museums, require a doctorate.

Education directors often earn a bachelor's degree in liberal arts, history, or one of the sciences.

They go on to earn a master's degree in a specialized area of education.

Earnings

Salaries for education directors vary depending on the size, type, and location of the institution, as well as the director's education and experience. The average beginning salary for education directors with bachelor's degrees and one year of experience is $23,000. Those with master's degrees may earn starting salaries of $33,000. The Association of Art Museum Directors reports that the average salaries for education directors are from $35,000 to $56,000 a year.

Outlook

The employment outlook for education directors is expected to increase more slowly than the average through 2008. Many museums and cultural institutions have cut their budgets and reduced the size of their education departments. Competition will be stiff for jobs in large cities and in well-known, popular institutions.

FOR MORE INFO

This organization provides information and training through publications, annual meetings, seminars, and workshops.
American Association for State and Local History
1717 Church Street
Nashville, TN 37203-2991
615-320-3203
http://www.aaslh.org

For a directory of internships offered through public gardens, contact:
American Association of Botanical Gardens and Arboreta
351 Longwood Road
Kenneth Square, PA 19348
610-925-2500
http://www.aabga.org

For a directory of museums and other information, contact:
American Association of Museums
1575 Eye Street, NW, Suite 400
Washington, DC 20005
202-289-1818
http://www.aam-us.org

RELATED JOBS

Librarians
Museum Directors and Curators
Museum Teachers
Museum Technicians
Naturalists
Teachers and Professors

Elementary School Teachers

What Elementary School Teachers Do

Elementary school teachers plan lessons, teach a variety of subjects, and keep student records. Elementary school usually includes kindergarten through the fifth grade.

Elementary teachers instruct about 20 to 30 students in the same grade. In the early grades, they teach basic skills in reading, writing, counting, and telling time. With older students, they teach history, geography, math, English, and handwriting. In some elementary schools, there are special teachers for art, music, and physical education.

Teachers use a variety of aids to instruct their students. These aids include the computer and Internet, textbooks, workbooks, magazines, newspapers, maps, charts, and posters. They use arts and crafts projects, music, science experiments, contests, and role-playing.

3M Company

An elementary school teacher teaches students about teeth using a lecture accompanied by audiovisual aids, followed by a discussion.

Teachers must have a love of learning and be enthusiastic about working with children. Some elementary school teachers work in multi-age classrooms, where students in a small age range are taught together. Others teach in bilingual classrooms where students are instructed in two languages throughout the day.

Before and after school, teachers spend time planning classes. They grade papers, tests, and homework assignments, and prepare student reports.

Teachers work with the school principal to solve problems, set up field trips, and plan school assemblies. They meet with parents to keep them informed about their

EXPLORING

• Your school may have a program for older students to tutor younger students in reading or math.
• Volunteer to teach Sunday school classes or become an assistant in a scout troop.
• Look for opportunities to coach children's athletic teams.
• Your local community theater may need directors and assistants for summer children's productions.
• Teach a younger sister or brother to read and write.

child's progress, and with school psychologists and social workers to help students with learning difficulties and other problems.

Education and Training

In high school, you should take advanced courses in English, math, science, history, and government.

All school teachers must be college graduates and must be certified by the state in which they want to teach. In college, you should major in education and take courses in the teaching of reading, the guidance of the young child, literature for children, and others. You will spend several weeks as a student teacher in an actual elementary school classroom. Your

A BRIEF HISTORY

The history of elementary education goes back to the people of Judah, who established schools for young children in synagogues about 100 BC, as part of the children's religious training.

In the early days of Western elementary education, the teacher only had to complete elementary school to be qualified to teach. School terms were generally about six months. The school building was often small, poorly heated, and badly lit. Many elementary schools combined all eight grades into one room, and the course of study was the same for everyone. In these early schools, the teacher was not well paid and had little recognition in the community.

When people decided that teachers should be better-educated, the normal school—a school designed to train teachers—was established. The first normal school, opened in Concord, Vermont, in 1823, was a private school. The first state-supported normal school was established in Lexington, Massachusetts, in 1839. By 1900, nearly every state had at least one state-supported normal school.

college program will lead to state certification. Some states may require you to take additional certification tests after graduating from an education program.

Earnings

According to the American Federation of Teachers, average beginning teachers with bachelor's degrees earned $26,600 a year in 1999. The average maximum earnings for teachers with master's degrees were $47,400. The U.S. Department of Labor reports that the 1998 median for K-12 teachers was between $33,600 and $37,900. Salaries ranged from $19,700 to $70,000 a year.

Outlook

The U.S. Department of Education predicts 1 million new teachers will be needed through 2008 to meet rising enrollments and to replace the large number of retiring teachers and those who quit teaching for other jobs. Better salaries will be needed to attract new

FOR MORE INFO

American Federation of Teachers
555 New Jersey Avenue, NW
Washington, DC 20001
202-879-4400
http://www.aft.org

National Education Association
1201 16th Street, NW
Washington, DC 20036
202-833-4000
http://www.nea.org

teachers, along with other changes such as smaller class sizes and safer schools. There will be a greater demand for teachers in inner-city schools and for those with specialties in math, science, and foreign language.

RELATED JOBS

Guidance Counselors
Preschool Teachers
Recreation Workers
School Administrators
Secondary School Teachers

ESL Teachers

English Isn't Easy

Less than four centuries ago, no more than a few million people spoke English. Today, it is the primary language of about a third of a billion people. English is spoken as a second language by tens of millions of others. However, English is considered one of the most difficult languages to learn, mainly because of its many irregularities. It has a larger vocabulary than any other language and uses numerous slang terms and newly coined words and phrases.

What ESL Teachers Do

English as a Second Language (ESL) teachers teach people of all ages the English language. Most students are immigrants and refugees. Some may be children of foreign-born parents, or children who may be living in a home where English is not spoken.

Many public and private schools employ ESL instructors. They do not necessarily speak the language of the students they are instructing. However, many teachers try to learn some key words and phrases in their students' native tongues in order to communicate better.

The main goal of ESL teachers is to help students learn to use the English language to communicate both verbally and in writing. In the classroom they use many different teaching methods including games, videos, computers, field trips, role-playing, and other activities to make learning fun and interesting. Classes often center on teaching conversation skills, telephone skills, the art of listening, and the idioms of the English language. The instructor helps students learn correct pronunciation, sentence structure, vocabulary, composition, and punctuation.

Many ESL teachers teach adults. With the steady flow of refugees and immigrants to the United States, community centers, libraries, churches, and assistance centers are offering ESL classes as well.

ESL teachers also find many opportunities overseas, teaching English as a foreign language. Some overseas employers offer free housing, medical care, and other benefits as part of the teaching contract.

Education and Training

Courses in English, foreign language, and social studies are highly recommended for ESL teachers. To teach in public schools, you must be a college graduate. A few schools offer a major in ESL. You may also major in education with a concentration in ESL as a subject area. Teachers in public schools must be licensed by the state in which they teach.

ESL teachers of adult students do not need a license. There are many training pro-

EXPLORING

• Join a foreign language club.

• Talk to your teachers and parents about becoming a foreign exchange student or housing a foreign exchange student.

• Participate in community multicultural events to learn more about other cultures and languages.

• Volunteer to help with any assistance programs that your community or church might have for immigrants or refugees.

Scholars believe that the English language is one of the most difficult languages to learn. What would you think if you moved to our country and you were trying to speak our language?

The words rough, bough, cough, though, and through all have the same endings, but think about how you pronounce each word.

Making words plural can really cause confusion. For instance, the plural of man is men, but the plural of can is cans. The plural of foot is feet, but the plural of root isn't "reet," but roots. The plural of mouse is mice, but the plural of blouse is blouses, not "blice."

We also have homonyms, which are words pronounced the same but mean different things. For example, foul and fowl; sight, cite, and site; hear and here; and to, two, and too.

Our language has a larger vocabulary than most others. For example, we can eat at a restaurant, a diner, a bistro, a grill, a luncheonette, a supper club, a coffee shop, a cafeteria, a buffet, or a cafe.

grams available for ESL teachers of adults. These programs usually last from four to 12 weeks. When you complete the program you receive a certificate or diploma.

Earnings

The American Federation of Teachers reports that the average salary for teachers is $39,347 a year. The average salary for a beginning teacher with a bachelor's degree is $26,600. The average salary for a teacher with a master's degree is $47,400 a year.

Earnings for ESL teachers overseas vary. Some positions are on a volunteer basis, where teachers receive no pay, but do receive housing, food, and transportation. Job assignments can vary in length from a few weeks to a year or more. Wages often depend on the country's economic health. Overseas teachers consider other benefits equal to pay, such as the opportunity to live and work in a foreign culture.

Outlook

According to the American Federation of Teachers, school districts report that there is a shortage of teachers of bilingual education. The increasing immigrant and refugee populations in the United States will create demand for instruction in the English language, whether in the school system, the community, or the workplace. Many community and social service agencies, as well as community colleges, are offering assistance to immigrants and refugees and will need ESL teachers.

The Bureau of Labor Statistics reports that the demand for adult education teachers is expected to grow as fast as the average for all occupations through the year 2008.

FOR MORE INFO

The following organizations provide information on ESL and other teaching careers.

American Federation of Teachers
555 New Jersey Avenue, NW
Washington, DC 20001
202-879-4400
http://www.aft.org

National Education Association
1201 16th Street, NW
Washington, DC 20036
202-833-4000
http://www.nea.org

TESOL (Teachers of English to Speakers of Other Languages, Inc.)
700 South Washington Street, Suite 200
Alexandria, VA 22314
703-836-0774
http://www.tesol.edu

Our Melting Pot

According to the 1990 U.S. Census, there are 327 languages spoken in America. After English, the most common languages are:

Spanish
French
German
Italian
Chinese

Tagalog
Polish
Korean
Vietnamese
Portuguese

Guidance Counselors

What Guidance Counselors Do

Guidance counselors help students with college, career, and personal choices. They help students to choose their classes and teachers and develop better study habits. They provide information and advice to students who are trying to select colleges and training programs. They supply necessary school records, write letters of recommendation, and guide students through the application process for admission and for financial aid.

Guidance counselors also help students who are having trouble with educational, social, or personal problems. Sometimes suggestions and encouragement are all that students need. But if a student has a serious problem, a counselor may refer the student to a social-welfare agency, child guidance clinic, health department, or other community-service agency.

Another important duty of guidance counselors is collecting and organizing materials for students to read on such topics as occupations, personal and social matters (for example, peer pressure and self-esteem), and educational opportunities beyond high school. They hold group guidance meetings with students in which topics of special interest to the group are discussed. They organize special days devoted to career exploration and college recruitment, inviting representatives of various occupations and colleges to the school to talk to students.

Guidance counselors help new students learn about the school and adjust to their new environment. They administer and grade standardized tests, and meet with parents, school psychologists, social workers, and other teachers to discuss individual students and school guidance programs.

Education and Training

To prepare for a career as a guidance counselor, take social studies, language arts, mathematics, and speech classes.

You need to earn a bachelor's degree and complete certain specified courses at the graduate level. About six out of ten guidance counselors have master's degrees.

EXPLORING

• These Web sites are examples of sites that a guidance counselor might suggest to high school students for college information:

Embark.com

PureAdvice.com

Collegebound.net

CollegeSurfing.com

OnlineCollegeFairs.com

• Volunteer to assist in the counselor's office, and help with career days and other events and programs.

RELATED JOBS

Adult and Vocational
Education Teachers
Elementary School Teachers
Rehabilitation Counselors
School Administrators
Secondary School Teachers

Graduate programs in counselor education include courses in career development, group counseling, and substance abuse counseling.

Most states require that counselors have a teaching certificate. You can earn a teaching certificate by taking classes during your undergraduate years.

Earnings

Wages for guidance counselors vary by region of the country, school and district size, and age of the students. Larger districts usually offer higher salaries, and counselors working with high school students tend to earn more than counselors for younger grades. The lowest salaries for guidance counselors in the United States are in the Southeast, and the highest are on the West Coast. Beginning salaries in the field average about $20,000, while the most experienced counselors can earn more than $74,000.

COUNSELORS OBJECT TO AD CAMPAIGN

North American Jaguar began an ad campaign on March 19, 2001, that showed a Jaguar with the message, "Your guidance counselor said you'd never amount to anything. Your guidance counselor drives a minivan." American School Counselor Association members found the ad demeaning to the profession of school counseling. In a letter to the president of North American Jaguar, ASCA Executive Director Richard Wong wrote, "We understand that your advertisement was meant to be humorous, and that you did not intend to undermine the profession, but many school counselors feel that the advertisement perpetuates a stereotype they have combated for years." Numerous school counselors sent letters of complaint to Jaguar as well.

On May 23, 2001, Jaguar Vice President of Public Affairs Simon Sproule notified Wong about Jaguar's decision to discontinue the ads. He also offered Jaguar's resources to help ASCA create a public relations campaign to promote professional school counseling.

According to the U.S. Department of Labor, the average salary for school counselors was $38,650 a year in 1998.

Outlook

The federal government has called for more counselors in the schools to help address issues of violence and other dangers, such as drug use. Though violence in the schools has been decreasing, the number of students afraid to go to school has increased. This increase is a result of the shootings and gang-related warfare that became headlines in the late 1990s. The government, along with counseling professionals, is also working to remove the stigma of mental illness, and to encourage more children and families to seek help from school counselors.

Technology will continue to assist counselors in their jobs. With Internet access in the

FOR MORE INFO

American Counseling Association
5999 Stevenson Avenue
Alexandria, VA 22304
703-823-9800
http://www.counseling.org

**American School
Counselor Association**
801 North Fairfax Street, Suite 310
Alexandria, VA 22314
703-683-2722
http://www.schoolcounselor.org

libraries, counselors can easily direct students to specific career information, scholarship applications, and college Web sites. School counselors may also follow the lead of Internet counselors and offer guidance online—students who want to be anonymous can request information and advice from counselors through email and other online services.

Math Teachers

What Math Teachers Do

Math teachers help students learn simple and advanced math theories and apply these concepts to everyday life.

Math teachers work in elementary, middle and high school classrooms. Some math teachers may also work as adult education teachers. Professors usually teach at the college level.

Math teachers teach complex mathematical subjects such as algebra, calculus, geometry, trigonometry, and statistics to middle and high school students. They may teach algebra to a class of ninth graders one period and trigonometry to high school seniors the next. Teachers must be able to get along with young people, have patience, and like to help others. They need good communication skills, since they often work with students from varying ethnic backgrounds and cultures.

Math teachers not only teach specific subjects, but they must make learning fun and teach students how to work together. Some schools use less structured classrooms to teach math skills, team problem solving, and cooperation. Math teachers encourage creative and logical thinking as it relates to math and education in general. They often use various teaching methods to keep students interested and help them learn. They may use games, computers, and experiments as hands-on teaching tools in the classroom. They may schedule field trips, guest speakers, or special events to show students how math skills are used in their daily lives and in the operation of businesses and government.

Math teachers also develop lesson plans, create exams, correct papers, calculate grades, and keep records. Some schools may also require teachers to lead extracurricular activities such as math clubs, competitions, and events. Teachers meet with and advise students, hold parent/teacher conferences, and attend faculty meetings. In addition, they may have to attend local, state, and national conferences. Teachers must take continuing education courses to maintain their teaching licenses.

EXPLORING

• Teach a younger sister or brother to count or do basic arithmetic, such as addition and subtraction. As they get a little older, you can teach them the value of coins and how to make change.

• Your school or community may have a volunteer program where you can tutor younger children in math.

• Here are some Web resources:
A+ Math
http://www.aplusmath.com/

AllMath
http://www.allmath.com

Just for Middle School Kids Math.com
http://www.kidsmath.com/

Education and Training

If you want to pursue a career as a math teacher, you should take high school math courses including algebra, geometry, trigonometry, and calculus. More advanced classes such as probability, statistics, and logic are also beneficial if they are available. Computer science, psychology, and English classes are also recommended.

Public school teachers in the United States and in the District of Columbia must be licensed. The state's board of education or a licensing committee usually grants this license. Although requirements for teaching licenses vary by state, all public schools require teachers to have a bachelor's degree and

How do these workers use math every day?

Architects
Auto Mechanics
Carpenters
Cooks and Chefs
Farmers
Fashion Designers
Graphic Designers
Photographers
Publishers
Real Estate Agents
Salespeople
Travel Agents

Did You Know?

Every 2-digit number that ends with a 9 is the sum of the multiple of the two digits plus the sum of the 2 digits.
For example, $29 = (2 \times 9) + (2 + 9)$.

And here's another amazing math mystery:

$$1 \times 8 + 1 = 9$$
$$12 \times 8 + 2 = 98$$
$$123 \times 8 + 3 = 987$$
$$1234 \times 8 + 4 = 9876$$
$$12345 \times 8 + 5 = 98765$$
$$123456 \times 8 + 6 = 987654$$
$$1234567 \times 8 + 7 = 9876543$$
$$12345678 \times 8 + 8 = 98765432$$
$$123456789 \times 8 + 9 = 987654321$$

complete the state's approved training program.

Earnings

The American Federation of Teachers reports that the average salary for teachers is $39,347 a year. The average salary for a beginning teacher with a bachelor's degree is $26,600. The average salary for a teacher with a master's degree is $47,400 a year.

The U.S. Department of Labor reports that the 1998 median for K-12 teachers was between $33,600 and $37,900. Salaries ranged from $19,700 to $70,000 a year.

Outlook

Teachers are generally in short supply across the nation due to rising school enrollments and the number of teachers who are retiring. The U.S. Department of Education predicts that 1 million new teachers will be needed by 2008. Math teachers are particularly needed. According to surveys conducted by AFT, school districts report a considerable shortage of math teachers, with greater shortages occurring in large cities.

FOR MORE INFO

American Federation of Teachers
555 New Jersey Avenue, NW
Washington, DC 20001
202-879-4400
http://www.aft.org

National Education Association
1201 16th Street, NW
Washington, DC 20036
202-833-4000
http://www.nea.org

The following association offers a packet of information regarding careers in mathematics.
National Council of Teachers of Mathematics
Department M
1906 Association Drive
Reston, VA 20191
703-620-9840
http://www.nctm.org

Museum Attendants and Teachers

What Museum Attendants and Teachers Do

Museum attendants protect museum collections and help museum visitors. They are sometimes called museum guards because they protect the exhibits from harm. They inform visitors of museum rules and regulations. Sometimes this means preventing patrons from touching a display, or warning children not to run through the halls. If an exhibit is popular and draws a large crowd, museum attendants keep everyone orderly.

In some museums, the attendants may have to check the thermostats and climate controls. A priceless document or work of art can be as easily destroyed by humid conditions as it can by careless hands. Attendants report any damage or needed repairs to the museum curator.

Museum attendants are the main source of information for museum visitors. They know about the exhibits as well as the

Children's Nature Museum is a special feature of the Academy of Natural Sciences of Philadelphia. Here a museum teacher teaches some youngsters about reptiles.

museum itself. Attendants answer questions from people of all ages and cultural backgrounds.

Most museums hold lectures, classes, workshops, and tours to teach the public about what is in the museum and why it is there. *Museum teachers* conduct all the educational programs. For special exhibits, the museum teacher works with the museum curator to develop written materials, such as pamphlets to be handed out at the display, books to be sold in the gift shop, or study guides for students. Museum teachers arrange and

EXPLORING

• Participate in museum programs, such as field trips, photography clubs, study groups, and behind-the-scenes tours.

• Talk to your local museum officials about any volunteer opportunities available.

WEIRD AND WACKY MUSEUMS

When you think of museums, you might first think of natural history, science, or art museums. But people have collected some strange items and opened museums to display them.

The Burlingame Museum of Pez, San Francisco, California, has hundreds of dispensers from the 1950s to the present.
http:/www.burlingamepezmuseum.com

The Banana Museum, Auburn, Washington, has nearly 4,000 banana-related items. http://www.geocities.com/napavalley/1799/

The Toaster Museum, Charlottesville, Virginia, not only has pop-up toasters, but toaster art, toys, and accessories. http://www.toaster.org

More weird museums are described in *Offbeat Museums: The Collections and Curators of America's Most Unusual Museums* by Saul Rubin (Santa Monica Press, 1997).

schedule classes for children and adults. They have strong communication skills and creativity to make these programs interesting to people of all ages and cultural backgrounds.

Education and Training

A high school diploma is required for museum atten-dants. Employers are more likely to hire those with college education or experience working in a museum. Attendants usually are trained on the job where they quickly learn about all the objects in the museum's permanent collection. They get additional training to learn about any special temporary exhibits.

Museum teachers need a college-level education with classes in both education and a specialty. For example, teachers in art museums have studied art history and education. Many colleges offer courses in museum studies (museology), which are valuable in the competitive field of museum work.

Earnings

Large museums in big cities pay more than smaller regional museums. Salaries for museum attendants range from $9,000 to $29,000 a year. The average salary for an educational assistant ranges from $22,000 to $32,000. An associate educator earns $36,000 on average. Museum teachers with experience who work in large museums earn about $44,000 a year.

Outlook

The education services provided by museum attendants and educators are an important part of a museum's operations. That means museums will expect greater professionalism, more

FOR MORE INFO

For information on careers, education and training, and internships, contact:
American Association of Museums
1575 Eye Street, NW, Suite 400
Washington, DC 20005
202-289-1818
http://www.aam-us.org

This association for anyone interested in art education has student memberships.
National Art Education Association
1916 Association Drive
Reston, VA 20191
703-860-8000
http://www.naea-reston.org

education, and specialization in the future for high-level positions. Since budgets are small and often unstable, museums will depend on volunteer attendants and teachers. Competition for paid jobs will be strong.

Music Teachers

What Music Teachers Do

Music teachers teach people how to sing, play musical instruments, and appreciate and enjoy the world of music. They teach private lessons and classes. They may work at home or in a studio, school, college, or conservatory. Many music teachers are also performing musicians.

Teachers help students learn to read music, develop their voices, breathe correctly, and hold and play their instruments properly. As their students master the techniques of their art, teachers guide them through more and more difficult pieces of music. Music teachers often organize recitals or concerts that feature their students. These recitals allow family and friends to hear how well the students are progressing and helps students get performing experience.

Private music teachers may teach children who are just beginning to play or sing, teens who hope to make music their

A music teacher teaches a variety of vocal techniques to a large choir.

career, or adults who are interested in music lessons for their own enjoyment.

Music teachers in elementary and secondary schools often offer group and private lessons. They direct in-school glee clubs, concert choirs, marching bands, or orchestras. College and university teachers are also frequently performers or composers. They divide their time between group and individual instruction and may teach several music subjects, such as music appreciation, music history, theory, and pedagogy (the teaching of music).

Education and Training

If you are interested in becoming a music teacher, you probably are already taking

EXPLORING

• Sing in your school or church choir. Join a band or orchestra. Get as much experience as you can playing, singing, and performing.
• Read all you can about music theory, music history, famous musicians, and performance.
• Talk to your music teachers about what they like and don't like about teaching music. Ask them how they became music teachers.

METHODS FOR TEACHING MUSIC

There are several well-known methods for teaching music to young children.

1. The **Suzuki** method of music education was begun in the mid-1900s by Japanese violinist Shinichi Suzuki (1898-1998). He believed that the best way to learn music is to be exposed to it from a very early age. He thought young children should learn to play an instrument in the same way that they learn to speak and read—by listening, absorbing, and copying.

In the beginning, the parent is given the first lessons on the instrument, while the child watches. In this way, the child becomes interested in copying the parent. When the child begins learning, it is by ear. Music reading is taught later, at about the same age a child learns to read books.

2. The **Orff-Schulwerk** system for teaching music to children was started by Carl Orff (1895-1982). It is based on rhythmic and verbal patterns and the pentatonic scale. Orff believed that music was connected with movement, dance, and speech.

Orff-Schulwerk uses poems, rhymes, games, songs, and dances as examples and basic materials. Improvisation and composition are key to learning and appreciating music.

3. The **Kodaly** philosophy is based on the work of Zoltan Kodaly (1882-1967). He believed it was important for children to sing, play instruments, and dance from memory. Children start learning traditional songs, games, chants, and folk songs and later learn music of other cultures and countries. The Kodaly method also involves performing, listening to, and analyzing the great art music of the world, as well as mastering musical skills, such as reading and writing music, singing, and part-singing.

voice lessons or are learning to play an instrument. Participation in music classes, choral groups, bands, and orchestras is also good preparation for a music teaching career.

Like all musicians, music teachers spend years mastering their instruments or developing their voices. Private teachers need no formal training or licenses, but most have spent years studying with an experienced musician, either in a school or conservatory or through private lessons.

Teachers in elementary schools and high schools must have a state-issued teaching license. There are about 600 conservatories, universities, and colleges that offer bachelor's degrees in music education to qualify students for state certificates.

To teach music in colleges and schools of music or in conservatories, you must usually have a graduate degree in music. However, very talented and well-known performers or composers are sometimes hired without any formal graduate training. Only a few people reach that level of fame.

Earnings

Salaries for music teachers vary depending on the type of teaching, the number of hours spent teaching, and the skill of the teacher. Private teachers who instruct beginning and intermediate students charge from $10 to $50 an hour. Public elementary school teachers earn average salaries of $37,000 a year. Public secondary school teachers earn about $39,100 a year.

Outlook

Opportunities for music teachers are expected to grow at an

FOR MORE INFO

National Association for Music Education
1806 Robert Fulton Drive
Reston, VA 20191
800-336-3768
http://www.menc.org

Music Teachers National Association
Carew Tower
441 Vine Street, Suite 505
Cincinnati, OH 45202-2814
http://www.mtna.org

average rate in elementary schools and colleges and universities, but at a slower rate in secondary schools. When schools face budget problems, music and other art programs are often the first to be cut. Competition has also increased as more instrumental musicians enter teaching because of the lack of performing jobs.

Naturalists

During the 19th century in the United States, many great forests were cut down and huge areas of land were leveled for open-pit mining and quarrying. More disease occurred with the increase of air pollution from the smokestacks of factories, home chimneys, and engine exhaust. At the same time there was a dramatic decrease in populations of elk, antelope, deer, bison, and other animals of the Great Plains. Some types of bear, cougar, and wolf became extinct, as well as several kinds of birds, such as the passenger pigeon. In the latter half of the 19th century, the government set up a commission to develop scientific management of fisheries. It established the first national park (Yellowstone National Park in Wyoming), and set aside the first forest reserves. These early steps led to the modern conservation movement.

What Naturalists Do

Naturalists study the natural world in order to learn the best way to preserve the earth and its living creatures—humans, animals, and plants. They teach the public about the environment and show people what they can do about such hazards as pollution.

Naturalists may work in wildlife museums, private nature centers, or large zoos. Some naturalists work for parks, most of which are operated by state or federal governments. Naturalists also can work as *nature resource managers, wildlife conservationists, ecologists,* and *environmental educators* for many different employers.

Depending on where they work, naturalists may protect and conserve wildlife or particular kinds of land, such as prairie or wetlands. Other naturalists research and carry out plans to restore lands that have been damaged by erosion, fire, or devel-

In the Everglades, this naturalist uses binoculars to view the many species of birds to be identified for a wetland report.

Thunder Mountain

opment. Some naturalists re-create wildlife habitats and nature trails. They plant trees, for example, or label existing plants. *Fish and wildlife wardens* help regulate populations of fish, hunted animals, and protected animals. They control hunting and fishing and make sure species are thriving but not overpopulating their territories. *Wildlife managers, range managers,* and *conservationists* also maintain the plant and animal life in a certain area. They work in parks or on ranges that have both domestic livestock and wild animals. They test soil and water for nutrients and pollution. They count plant and animal populations each season.

Naturalists do some indoor work. They raise funds for projects, write reports,

EXPLORING

• Visit your local nature centers and park preserves often. Attend any classes or special lectures they offer. There may be opportunities to volunteer to help clean up sites, plant trees, or maintain pathways and trails.
• Hiking, birdwatching, and photography are good hobbies for future naturalists.
• Get to know your local wildlife. What kind of insects, birds, fish, and other animals live in your area? Your librarian will be able to help you find books that identify local flora and fauna.

keep detailed records, and write articles, brochures, and newsletters to educate the public about their work. They might campaign for support for protection of an endangered species by holding meetings and hearings. Other public education activities include giving tours and nature walks and holding demonstrations, exhibits, and classes.

Education and Training

Naturalists must have at least a bachelor's degree in biology, zoology, chemistry, botany, natural history, or environmental science. A master's degree is not a requirement, but is useful, and many naturalists have a master's degree in education. Experience gained through summer jobs and volunteer work can be just as important as educational requirements.

Experience working with the public is also helpful.

Earnings

Starting salaries for full-time naturalists range from about

SOME PIONEER NATURALISTS

Ralph Waldo Emerson (1803-1882) was an American philosopher and author. He helped form and promote the philosophy known as Transcendentalism, which emphasizes the spiritual dimension in nature and in all persons.

Henry David Thoreau (1817-1862) was an American author. His *Walden* (1854) is a classic of American literature. It tells about the two years he lived in a small cabin on the shore of Walden Pond near Concord, Massachusetts. In *Walden*, he described the changing seasons and other natural events and scenes that he observed.

Gilbert White (1720-1793) was an English minister. While living and working in his native village of Selborne (southwest of London), White became a careful observer of its natural setting. He corresponded with important British naturalists and eventually published *The Natural History and Antiquities of Selborne*.

$15,000 to $22,000 per year. Some part-time workers, however, make as little as minimum wage ($5.15 per hour). For some positions, housing and vehicles may be provided. Earnings vary for those with added responsibilities or advanced degrees. Field officers and supervisors make between $25,000 and $45,000 a year, and upper management employees can earn between $30,000 and $70,000.

Outlook

In the next decade, the job outlook for naturalists is expected to be only fair, despite the public's increasing environmental awareness. Private nature centers and preserves—where forests, wetlands, and prairies are restored—are continuing to open in the United States, but possible government cutbacks in nature programs may limit their growth. Competition will be quite high, since there are many qualified people entering this field.

FOR MORE INFO

Bureau of Land Management
U.S. Department of the Interior
1849 C Street, Room 406-LS
Washington, DC 20240
http://www.blm.gov/

Environmental Careers Organization
179 South Street
Boston, MA 02111
http://www.eco.org

This group has an international computer network called EcoNet that features electronic bulletin boards on environmental issues, services, events, news, and job listings.
Institute for Global Communication
18 DeBoom Street
San Francisco, CA 94107
415-442-0220
http://www.econet.org

National Wildlife Federation
8925 Leesburg Pike
Vienna, VA 22184
718-790-4000
http://www.nwf.org

North American Association for Environmental Education
410 Tarvin Road
Rock Spring, GA 30739
706-764-2926
http://naaee.org

Preschool Teachers

Storytime

Here are some recent books for preschool children. Each book addresses a basic aspect of development:

Colors: *Hello, Red Fox* by Eric Carle (Simon and Schuster, 1998). This is a story about a party tossed by Mama Frog and her confusion over the changing colors of her guests.

Senses: *What Do You See When You Shut Your Eyes?* by Cynthia Zarin and Sarah Durham (Houghton Mifflin, 1998). The book asks questions that invite children to think about their senses and sensibilities.

Counting: *My Little Sister Ate One Hare* by Bill Grossman and Kevin Hawkes (Random House, 1998). A little sister begins with one hare and moves on to devour nine lizards. The sing-song rhyming helps children learn their numbers with humorous and colorful illustrations.

What Preschool Teachers Do

Preschool teachers teach children who are between three and five years old. They work in child care centers, nursery schools, Head Start programs, and other private and public programs. They prepare children for kindergarten and grade school by teaching letters, numbers, colors, days of the week, and how to tell time. Preschool teachers also introduce children to books, educational games, and computer software for children. Teachers of two-, three-, and four-year-old children teach students social skills through play and activities. Kindergarten teachers focus more on numbers, words, and writing to prepare students for grade school math, spelling, and reading.

In preschool classrooms, teachers plan and lead activities like storytelling, arts and crafts projects, and singing, depending on the abilities and interests of the children. For example, to teach children

First United Methodist Day Care, Champaign, Illinois

A preschool teacher comforts a student who was upset during playtime.

about the senses, telling time, or writing the alphabet, they might use finger-painting, puppets, music, or games. Teachers have to think about which skills children should be learning at a particular age. They encourage the children to think creatively and to express their feelings and ideas. They help them develop social skills as they get used to being in school with other children, and introduce them to the concepts of sharing and playing in groups. Other social skills might include manners, hygiene, and how to clean up after themselves.

Preschool teachers also get to know the children's parents and regularly provide them with reports on progress and behavior. They might also invite parents along

EXPLORING

• There are many volunteer opportunities for working with kids. Check with your library or local literacy program about tutoring children and reading to preschoolers.

• Summer day camps or church schools with preschool classes may offer assistant or aide opportunities.

• Baby-sitting is a good way to get child care experience.

• Teach a younger sister or brother letters, numbers, and colors. Help them learn to read or tell time.

YOUNG CHILDREN LEARN THROUGH WORK

Young children can do many chores around the house that teach them to be responsible and independent. Christine A. Readdick and Kathy Douglas, authors of "More Than Line Leader and Door Holder: Engaging Young Children in Real Work," an article in the journal, *Young Children,* say children are eager to help adults and work is an important part of early learning.

Some people object to making children work, but Readdick and Douglas suggest that children can learn a lot from helping to gather, prepare, and cook food; running errands; doing light housekeeping chores; caring for pets; or gardening.

on field trips, and to the classroom to observe.

Education and Training

Large child care centers sometimes hire high school graduates who have some child care experience and give them on-the-job training. For example, American Montessori Society offers a career program that requires a three-month training period followed by a year of supervised on-the-job training.

Some schools require preschool teachers to have bachelor's

degrees. There are many colleges and universities that offer programs in early childhood education and child care. In some states, preschool teachers are required to be licensed. The Child Development Associate credential qualifies a person to teach preschool in some states. Kindergarten teachers must have education degrees and state certification.

Earnings

Salaries in this profession tend to be lower than for teaching positions in public elementary and high schools. Because some preschool programs are only in the morning or afternoon, many preschool teachers work only part-time. As part-time workers, preschool teachers may earn minimum wage ($5.15 an hour) to start.

According to the U.S. Department of Labor, preschool teachers earned about $17,310 a year in 1998. Salaries ranged from $12,000 to $30,300. Kindergarten teachers, on average, have the highest salaries in this field, earning about the same as elementary school teachers (about $23,300 in 1997).

Outlook

Employment opportunities for preschool teachers are expected to increase faster than the average through 2008, according to the U.S. Department of Labor. Specific job opportunities vary from state to state. Jobs should be available at private child care centers, nursery schools, Head Start facilities, public and private kinder-

FOR MORE INFO

For more information about preschool teachers and child care workers, contact:
National Association for the Education of Young Children
1509 16th Street, NW
Washington, DC 20036
800-424-2460
http://www.naeyc.org

To learn more about CDA certification, contact the following organization:
Council for Early Childhood Professional Recognition
2460 16th Street, NW
Washington, DC 20009
800-424-4310
http://www.cdacouncil.org

For information on training programs, contact:
American Montessori Society
281 Park Avenue South, 6th Floor
New York, NY 10010-6102
212-358-1250
http://www.amshq.org

gartens, and laboratory schools connected with universities and colleges. In the past, the majority of preschool teachers were female, and although this continues to be the case, more males are becoming involved in early childhood education.

School Administrators

The E-Rate

According to the National Center for Education Statistics, wealthy schools in the late 1990s were more than twice as likely to have Internet access in classrooms than poor schools. Schools with high minority enrollment were almost three times less likely than predominately white schools to have Internet access.

Due to this technology gap, the FCC ruled in 1997 to provide all K-12 schools and public libraries up to $2.25 billion a year in discounts, called E-Rates, for telecommunications services. The average E-Rate is about 60 percent. The poorest schools receive discounts of 80 to 90 percent.

What School Administrators Do

School administrators oversee the operation of schools or entire school districts. They work with either public or private schools. Those who work as administrators in private schools are often called *headmasters* (or *headmistresses*) or *school directors.* They make sure students, teachers, and other employees follow educational guidelines and meet budget requirements.

There are two basic kinds of school administrators in public schools: principals and superintendents. School *principals* supervise teachers and make sure they are using approved teaching methods. They visit classrooms and examine learning materials. They also supervise the school's counselors and other staff members. They review the students' performance and decide how to handle students with learning or behavior problems. In larger schools, they may be aided by *assistant principals,* sometimes called *deans of students.*

School *superintendents* are responsible for an entire school district. They are appointed by the board of education to see that the district's schools meet their standards. Superintendents have many duties. They hire staff, settle labor disputes, make out the district's budget, oversee school bus service, speak to community groups, purchase school supplies, and make sure school buildings are maintained and repaired.

Education and Training

Most principals and assistant principals have had years of teaching experience and hold master's degrees in educational administration. Guidance counselors, resource center directors, and other staff members also may work up to the position of principal. Most states require school principals to be licensed, but licensing requirements vary from state to state. Private schools are not subject to state certification requirements, so some private school principals and assistant principals may hold only a bachelor's degree. Most, however, have a master's degree.

EXPLORING

Before you can become a principal or superintendent, you need teaching experience. You can gain experience in education by:

• teaching Sunday school classes

• working as a summer camp counselor or day care center aide

• working with a scouting group

• volunteering to coach a youth athletic team

• tutoring younger students

A doctorate in educational administration is often required for school superintendents. Large school districts may also want their superintendents to have a law or business degree. All school superintendents need to have previous experience as administrators in some field.

Earnings

The U.S. Department of Labor reports that median annual earnings of education administrators in 1998 were $60,400 a year. Salaries ranged from less than $30,480 to more than $92,680.

The Educational Research Service conducted a survey of the salaries of public school administrators for the 1997-98 school year. Assistant principals earned an average of $53,200 a year in elementary schools, and $61,000 a year in high schools. Elementary school principals earned about $65,000 a year, while high school principals earned $74,000. The average annual salary for a deputy superintendent was $99,000. Superintendents earned annual salaries of $106,000. Superintendents of large school districts (25,000 or more pupils)

WOMEN IN SCHOOL ADMINISTRATION

According to studies by the American Association of School Administrators, the number of women school superintendents has more than doubled in the last decade, from 6 percent to more than 14 percent. There are 1,974 women superintendents nationwide. The study also showed that more than half of the students in education administration programs are women.

Most school superintendent positions are filled by former teachers. According to the National Education Association, almost 75 percent of public school teachers are women. That means that 86 percent of school superintendents are chosen from 25 percent of the teaching pool.

can earn more than $130,000 a year.

Outlook

The American Association of School Administrators (AASA) reports that 6,000 school superintendents will need to be replaced over the next five years because of retirement or job changes. There is a shortage of qualified candidates to fill those positions. One reason is education: more than half (54 percent) of working superintendents don't have doctoral degrees, but many school boards prefer candidates with doctorates. Another reason for the shortage is that qualified people view school administration as too political, the pay is low, and there are restrictions on moving between districts.

AASA reports that a new career is developing to handle the shortage. A number of districts have hired interim superintendents as temporary replacements until they can find a permanent candidate.

FOR MORE INFO

American Association of School Administrators
1801 North Moore Street
Arlington, VA 22209
703-528-0700
http://www.aasa.org

National Association of Secondary School Principals
1904 Association Drive
Reston, VA 20191
703-860-0200
http://www.nassp.org

National Association of Elementary School Principals
1615 Duke Street
Alexandria, VA 22314
http://www.naesp.org

RELATED JOBS

Adult and Vocational Education Teachers
College Administrators
College Professors
Guidance Counselors
Special Education Teachers

Secondary School Teachers

The First Secondary Schools

Early secondary education was typically based upon training students to enter the clergy. Benjamin Franklin pioneered the idea of the academy, a broader secondary education that offered a flexible curriculum and a wide variety of academic subjects.

It was not until the 19th century that children of different social classes commonly attended school into the secondary grades. The first English Classical School was established in 1821, in Boston.

The junior high school was the idea of Dr. Charles W. Eliot, president of Harvard. In 1888, he recommended that secondary studies be started two years earlier than was the custom. The first junior high school opened in 1908, in Columbus, Ohio.

By the early 20th century, secondary school attendance was made mandatory in the United States.

What Secondary School Teachers Do

Secondary school teachers instruct junior and senior high school students. They usually specialize in a certain subject, such as English, mathematics, biology, or history, or they may teach several subjects. In addition to classroom instruction, they plan lessons, prepare tests, grade papers, complete report cards, meet with parents, and supervise other activities. They often meet individually with students to discuss homework assignments, or academic or personal problems.

Depending on the subject, teachers may use lectures, films, photographs, readings, guest speakers, discussions, or demonstrations, to name a few teaching techniques. They interact with the students and ask and answer questions to make sure everyone understands the lessons. In order to reinforce the material taught in class, they assign homework, give tests, and assign projects that help

A secondary school teacher explains a science project to his students.

IBM

students develop an understanding of the material. Each subject has its own teaching requirements. For example, science teachers supervise laboratory projects where students work with microscopes and other equipment, and shop teachers teach students to use tools and building materials. Art teachers teach students to use paints, various sculpture media, or darkroom equipment.

Some secondary school teachers are specially trained to work with students who have disabilities. Others teach advanced lessons for students with high grades and achievement scores.

Secondary school teachers have many responsibilities outside of the classroom,

EXPLORING

Volunteer for a peer tutoring program. Other opportunities that will give you teaching experience include coaching an athletic team at the YMCA/YWCA, counseling at a summer camp, teaching an art course at a community center, or assisting with a community theater production.

school newspaper, or the drama club.

Education and Training

Secondary school teachers must have at least a bachelor's degree in an approved teacher training program. Many colleges and universities offer these programs in their education departments. You must take courses in the subject area you want to teach, as well as a number of education courses covering teaching techniques and related subjects. You must also spend several months as a student teacher under the supervision of an experienced teacher. Upon completion of the program, you receive certification as a secondary school teacher. Many teachers go on to earn master's degrees in education.

All teachers must be certified before beginning work, and many school systems require additional qualifications. While

SALARY TIMELINE

The American Federation of Teachers' first salary survey in 1948-49 polled 1.25 million teachers. Salaries averaged under $3,000 a year.

During the 1960s, wages for teachers increased. In 1964-65, the national average salary for a teacher was $6,195. By 1972-73, the national average teacher salary increased to $10,176.

Today, the average salary for 2.8 million teachers is $40,574, tens of thousands of dollars less per year than their peers earn in other professions. These low salaries are having a serious impact on the ability of school districts around the country to attract the best candidates into the teaching profession.

as well. They keep grade and attendance records. They prepare lesson plans, exams, and homework assignments. In between classes, they oversee study halls and supervise lunchroom activities. They attend school meetings or meet with parents and students. They may supervise extracurricular activities like sports teams, the working, teachers must often attend education conferences and summer workshops to maintain certification and further their training.

Earnings

According to the U.S. Department of Labor, the median annual salary for kindergarten, elementary, and secondary school teachers was between $33,600 and $37,900 in 1998. Salaries ranged from $19,700 to $70,000 a year.

The American Federation of Teachers 1999 survey found that the average beginning salary for a teacher with only a bachelor's degree was $26,639. The average maximum salary for a teacher with a master's degree was $47,439.

Outlook

The U.S. Department of Educaiton predicts that 322,000 more secondary teachers will be needed by 2008. The National Education Association believes this will be a challenge

FOR MORE INFO

American Federation of Teachers
555 New Jersey Avenue, NW
Washington, DC 20001
202-879-4400
http://www.aft.org

National Education Association
1201 16th Street, NW
Washington, DC 20036
202-833-4000
http://www.nea.org

because of the low salaries that are paid to secondary school teachers. Higher salaries will be necessary to attract new teachers and retain experienced ones, along with other changes such as smaller classroom sizes and safer schools. Other challenges for the profession involve attracting more men into teaching. The percentage of male secondary school teachers continues to decline.

Special Education Teachers

What Special Education Teachers Do

Special education teachers work with students who need special attention, including those who have physical, developmental, behavioral, or learning disabilities, as well as those who are gifted and talented. They create individual programs for each student. They work closely with students to determine their learning and skill levels, and they work with school psychologists, social workers, occupational and physical therapists, and speech-language therapists.

Some students have learning disabilities that prevent them from learning through usual teaching methods. They may need instruction at a slower pace or to work in quiet, nondistracting settings. Teachers may need to read assignments aloud to them, and help them focus their attention on school work.

Some students have emotional or behavioral problems. Others are considered below average in their mental abilities. Some students are language impaired, which means they have trouble communicating. Special education teachers work with students who are visually impaired or blind, and hard of hearing or deaf. They also help students with physical handicaps such as muscle, nerve, or bone disorders. When working with physically handicapped students, teachers may use special equipment, such as computers that are operated by touching a screen or by voice commands, or books in Braille.

Most special education teachers work in public schools. Some, however, work in local education agencies, colleges and universities, and private schools. They may spend their days in specially equipped classrooms, ordinary classrooms, therapy rooms, and clinics.

Education and Training

College preparatory courses in English, science, math, and government will help you prepare for this career. Speech courses will develop good communication skills and psychology courses will help you understand some of the learning problems your students face.

EXPLORING

• Become involved in a school or community mentoring program for students with special needs. There may also be other opportunities for volunteer work or part-time jobs with community agencies, camps, and residential facilities.

• Get to know special-needs students at your school.

• Learn to use sign language or read Braille.

• To learn more about disability issues, visit this Web site, which has links to a variety of resources: http://soeweb.syr.edu/thechp/disres.htm. Also visit *Ragged Edge* online, a magazine that covers the disability experience in America: http://www.ragged-edge-mag.com.

The requirements for becoming a special education teacher are similar to those for becoming an elementary or secondary school teacher, but may involve a longer period of training. All states require teachers to earn a bachelor's degree that includes specific education courses. Many states require an additional year or two of graduate study and some states require a master's degree in special education. You also must be certified by your state, which may involve passing an exam. In addition, you must complete one or more semesters of student teaching in order to gain firsthand experience in a classroom under the guidance of a certified teacher.

Earnings

According to the National Education Association, the average salary for special education teachers in 1998 was $37,850. According to the U.S. Department of Labor, salaries ranged from less than $25,450 to more

SPECIAL ED LETTERS

ADA: Americans with Disabilities Act

ADD: Attention Deficit Disorder

ADHD: Attention Deficit Hyperactivity Disorder

ASL: American Sign Language

B/VI: Blind/Visually Impaired

CLD: Culturally or Linguistically Different

DD: Developmentally Delayed

D/HI: Deaf/Hearing Impaired

ED: Emotionally Disturbed

IDEA: Individuals with Disabilities Educational Act

IEP: Individualized Education Plan

LD: Learning Disabled

MG: Mentally Gifted

MR: Mental Retardation

NI: Neurologically Impaired

OHI: Other Health Impaired

PH: Physically Handicapped

than $78,000. Public secondary schools paid an average of $39,000 and elementary schools, $38,000 a year. Private school teachers usually earn less compared to public school teachers.

Outlook

The field of special education is expected to grow faster than the average through 2008, according to the U.S. Department of Labor. This demand is caused partly by the growth in the number of special education students needing services. Because of the rise in the number of youths with disabilities under the age of 21, the government has approved more federally funded programs. Growth of jobs in this field has also been influenced positively by legislation in favor of training and employment for individuals with disabilities and a growing public awareness and interest in those with disabilities.

FOR MORE INFO

National Clearinghouse for Professions in Special Education
Council for Exceptional Children
1110 North Glebe Road, Suite 300
Arlington, VA 22201-5704
800-641-7824
http://www.special-ed-careers.org

National Education Association
1201 16th Street, NW
Washington, DC 20036
202-833-4000
http://www.nea.org

U.S. Department of Education
Office of Special Education and
Rehabilitative Services
400 Maryland Avenue, SW
Washington, DC 20202-0498
800-872-5327
http://www.ed.gov/offices/OSERS/
index.html

RELATED JOBS

Elementary School Teachers
ESL Teachers
Orientation and Mobility Specialists
Preschool Teachers
Secondary School Teachers
Sign Language Interpreters
Teacher Aides

Teacher Aides

What Teacher Aides Do

Teachers plan and teach lessons, grade papers, prepare exams, attend faculty meetings, and perform a variety of other duties. *Teacher aides* assist them in many of their responsibilities. Teacher aides are sometimes called *education paraprofessionals* or *paraeducators.*

Teacher aides help prepare instructional materials for students, assist students with their classroom work, and supervise lunchrooms, playgrounds, hallways, and other areas around the school. They also do paperwork, grade students' tests, and operate audiovisual equipment. They take attendance and distribute materials such as books, photocopies, and writing supplies.

Teacher aides make sure students get on the correct school bus after school ends and they stay with other students until parents and carpool drivers arrive. They help teachers with filing, word processing, and photocopying. Aides write requests for classroom supplies and help arrange class trips.

Teacher aides do some teaching. They give lectures, conduct group discussions, and listen to elementary school children read. They help run school projects, such as science fairs or theater productions and assist teachers on field trips to museums and zoos.

Teacher aides work in traditional schools and classrooms, in special education, bilingual education, and a variety of other settings. They most often work in elementary schools, but teacher aides also work in high schools, often with students who have learning disabilities or behavioral disorders. They often work in classes that have a large number of students or that have one or more students with disabilities.

Education and Training

To be a teacher aide, you need a well-rounded education in math, English, science, art, and physical education. Courses in child development, home economics, and sociology are valuable in this career. Educational requirements for teacher aides vary widely. Teacher aides

EXPLORING

• Volunteer to help with religious education classes at your place of worship.

• Volunteer to help with scouting troops or work as a counselor at a summer day camp.

• Volunteer to help coach a children's athletic team or work with children in after-school programs at community centers.

• Baby-sitting will give you experience in working with children and help you learn about the different stages of child development.

RELATED JOBS

Child Care Workers
College Professors
Elementary School Teachers
Preschool Teachers
Secondary School Teachers
Special Education Teachers

who handle clerical or supervisory duties only need a high school diploma. If you will be doing any teaching or classroom work, however, some college work is usually required.

Teacher aides often receive on-the-job training, usually under the supervision of a certified teacher.

Sometimes certified teachers work as teacher aides when they are new graduates, between jobs, or when they have moved to a new area and are unsure of where they want to apply for a teaching job.

Earnings

Teacher aides are usually paid on an hourly basis and usually only during the nine or ten months of the school calendar. Salaries vary depending upon the school or district, region of the country, and the duties the aides perform. Some teacher aides may earn as little as minimum wage ($5.15 an hour) while others earn up to $11.27 an hour, according to the U.S. Department of Labor. Median average annual salaries for teacher aides were $7.61 an hour in 1998. A study by the

Educational Research Service found that the average wage of an aide with teaching responsibilities was $9.04 an hour.

Outlook

Growth in this field is expected to be much faster than the average because of an expected increase in the number of school-age children. The U.S. Department of Labor predicts that this field will grow by 31 percent, or 375,000 jobs, between 1998 and 2008.

As the number of students in schools increases, new schools and classrooms will be added and more teachers and teacher aides will be hired. An expected shortage of teachers means that administrators will hire more aides to help with larger classrooms.

Because of increased responsibilities for aides, state departments of education will likely establish standards of training in the near future. The National Resource Center for Parapro-

FOR MORE INFO

To learn about current issues affecting paraprofessionals in education, contact:
American Federation of Teachers
555 New Jersey Avenue, NW
Washington, DC 20001
202-879-4400
http://www.aft.org

To order publications and to read current research and other information, contact:
Association for Childhood Education International
17904 Georgia Avenue, Suite 215
Olney, MD 20832
301-570-2111
http://www.udel.edu/bateman/acei

For information about training programs and other resources, contact:
National Resource Center for Paraprofessionals in Education and Related Services
Utah State University
6526 Old Main Hill
Logan, UT 84322-6526
435-797-7272
http://www.nrcpara.org

fessionals in Education and Related Services is currently designing national standards for paraeducator training.

Glossary

accredited: Approved as meeting established standards for providing good training and education. This approval is usually given by an independent organization of professionals to a school or a program in a school. Compare **certified** and **licensed**.

apprentice: A person who is learning a trade by working under the supervision of a skilled worker. Apprentices often receive classroom instruction in addition to their supervised practical experience.

apprenticeship: 1. A program for training apprentices (see apprentice). 2. The period of time when a person is an apprentice. In highly skilled trades, apprenticeships may last three or four years.

associate's degree: An academic rank or title granted by a community or junior college or similar institution to graduates of a two-year program of education beyond high school.

bachelor's degree: An academic rank or title given to a person who has completed a four-year program of study at a college or university. Also called an undergraduate degree or baccalaureate.

certified: Approved as meeting established requirements for skill, knowledge, and experience in a particular field. People are certified by the organization of professionals in their field. Compare **accredited** and **licensed**.

community college: A public two-year college, attended by students who do not live at the college. Graduates of a community college receive an associate degree and may transfer to a four-year college or university to complete a bachelor's degree. Compare **junior college** and **technical college**.

diploma: A certificate or document given by a school to show that a person has completed a course or has graduated from the school.

doctorate: An academic rank or title (the highest) granted by a graduate school to a person who has completed a two- to three-year program after having received a master's degree.

fringe benefit: A payment or benefit to an employee in addition to regular wages or salary. Examples of fringe benefits include a pension, a paid vacation, and health or life insurance.

graduate school: A school that people may attend after they have received their bachelor's degree. People who complete an educational program at a graduate school earn a master's degree or a doctorate.

intern: An advanced student (usually one with at least some college training) in a professional field who is employed in a job that is intended to provide supervised practical experience for the student.

internship: 1. The position or job of an intern (see intern). 2. The period of time when a person is an intern.

junior college: A two-year college that offers courses like those in the first half of a four-year college program. Graduates of a junior college usually receive an associate degree and may transfer to a four-year college or university to complete a bachelor's degree. Compare **community college.**

liberal arts: The subjects covered by college courses that develop broad general knowledge rather than specific occupational skills. The liberal arts are often considered to include philosophy, literature and the arts, history, language, and some courses in the social sciences and natural sciences.

licensed: Having formal permission from the proper authority to carry out an activity that would be illegal without that permission. For example, a person may be licensed to practice medicine or to drive a car. Compare **certified**.

major: (in college) The academic field in which a student specializes and receives a degree.

master's degree: An academic rank or title granted by a graduate school to a person who has completed a one- or two-year program after having received a bachelor's degree.

pension: An amount of money paid regularly by an employer to a former employee after he or she retires from working.

private: 1. Not owned or controlled by the government (such as private industry or a private employment agency). 2. Intended only for a particular person or group; not open to all (such as a private road or a private club).

public: 1. Provided or operated by the government (such as a public library). 2. Open and available to everyone (such as a public meeting).

regulatory: Having to do with the rules and laws for carrying out an activity. A regulatory agency, for example, is a government organization that sets up required procedures for how certain things should be done.

scholarship: A gift of money to a student to help the student pay for further education.

social studies: Courses of study (such as civics, geography, and history) that deal with how human societies work.

starting salary: Salary paid to a newly hired employee. The starting salary is usually a smaller amount than is paid to a more experienced worker.

technical college: A private or public college offering two- or four-year programs in technical subjects. Technical colleges offer courses in both general and technical subjects and award associate degrees and bachelor's degrees.

technician: A worker with specialized practical training in a mechanical or scientific subject who works under the supervision of scientists, engineers, or other professionals. Technicians typically receive two years of college-level education after high school.

technologist: A worker in a mechanical or scientific field with more training than a technician. Technologists typically must have between two and four years of college-level education after high school.

undergraduate: A student at a college or university who has not yet received a degree.

undergraduate degree: See **bachelor's degree**.

union: An organization whose members are workers in a particular industry or company. The union works to gain better wages, benefits, and working conditions for its members. Also called a labor union or trade union.

vocational school: A public or private school that offers training in one or more skills or trades. Compare **technical college**.

wage: Money that is paid in return for work done, especially money paid on the basis of the number of hours or days worked.

Index of Job Titles

Teaching
on the Web

All About Teaching

http://www.recruitingteachers.org/aboutteach/index.html

American Federation of Teachers

http://www.aft.org

AskEric

http://ericir.syr.edu/about

The History of Education and Childhood

http://www.socsci.kun.nl/ped/whp/histeduc

National Center for Education Statistics

http://nces.ed.gov

National Education Association

http://www.nea.org

Teach-nology

http://www.teach-nology.com/

U.S. Department of Education

http://www.ed.gov

For Kendall

A RIVERBANK PRESS BOOK

This edition produced for
LONGMEADOW PRESS
201 High Ridge Road
Stamford, CT 06904

Printed and bound in Hong Kong/Jade Productions, Ltd.
THE BRAMBLEBERRYS is a Trademark of Riverbank Press

ISBN 0-681-40163-X

THE
BRAMBLEBERRYS
ANIMAL BOOK OF
COLORS

Created by
Marianna Mayer
and
Gerald McDermott

A RIVERBANK PRESS BOOK

LONGMEADOW PRESS

WHITE

RED

BLACK

GREEN

YELLOW

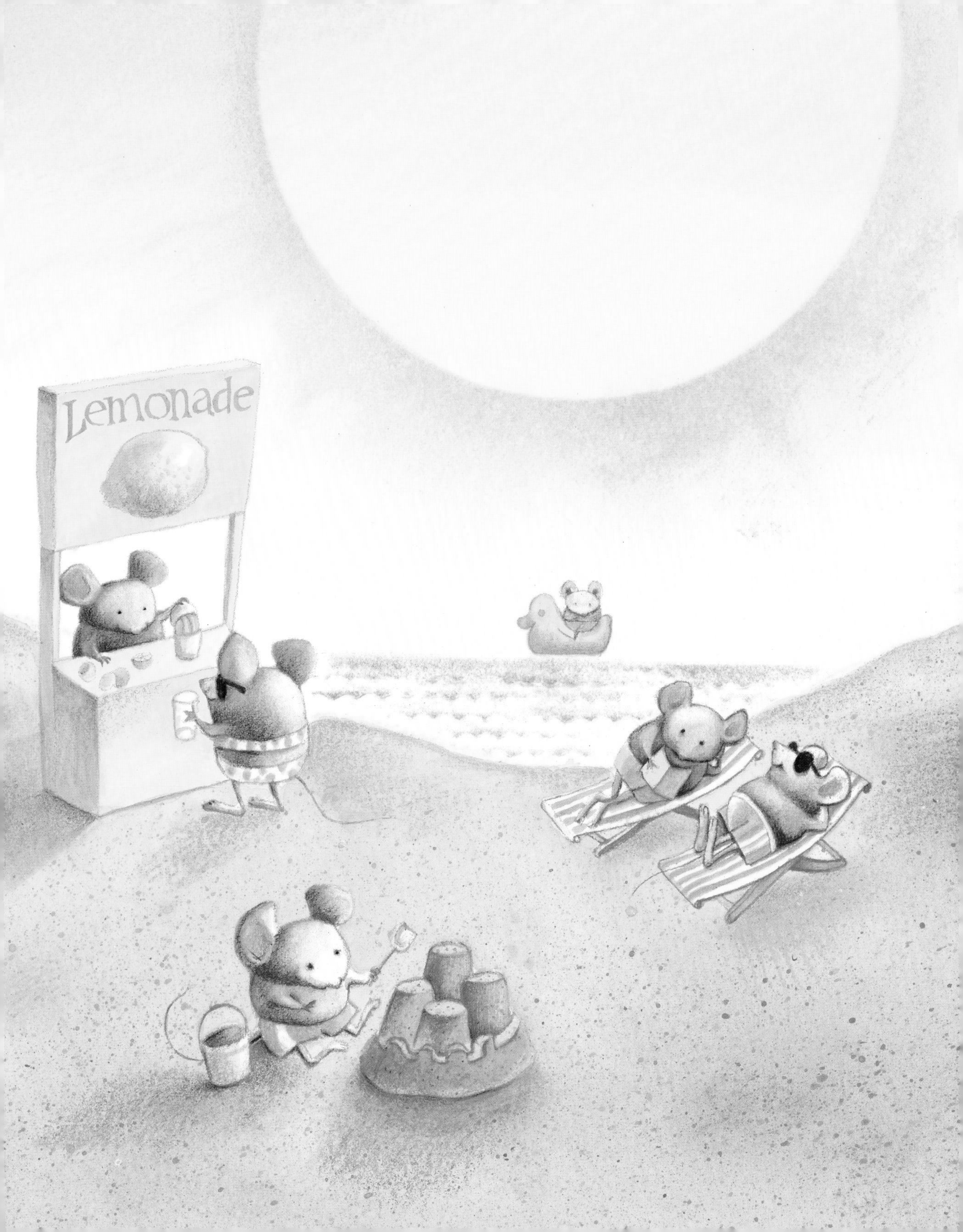
Lemonade

ORANGE

BROWN

GRAY

PINK